T0419580

The trains are called Big Boys, but traditionally locomotives are referred to as "she" by their engineers and crews. I have followed that tradition in my story, referring to this iconic locomotive as "she."

—Marsha Diane Arnold

Dedicated to Ed Dickens, the Steam Team,
and locomotive lovers around the world
—Marsha

For Felix
—AG

Text Copyright © 2025 Marsha Diane Arnold
Illustration Copyright © 2025 Adam Gustavson
Design Copyright © 2025 Sleeping Bear Press

SLEEPING BEAR PRESS™

2395 South Huron Parkway, Suite 200, Ann Arbor, MI 48104
www.sleepingbearpress.com © Sleeping Bear Press

Printed and bound in the United States.
10 9 8 7 6 5 4 3 2 1

Library of Congress Control Number: 2024034959
ISBN: 978-1-53411-314-5

BIG BOY 4014

AND THE STEAM TEAM

THE WORLD'S LARGEST STEAM ENGINE ROARS BACK TO LIFE!

BY **MARSHA DIANE ARNOLD** AND ILLUSTRATED BY **ADAM GUSTAVSON**

PUBLISHED BY SLEEPING BEAR PRESS™

If steam locomotives could dream, Big Boy would be pulling out of the station.

ChugaChuga . . . ChugaChuga . . . ChugaChuga . . . ChugaChug

If steam locomotives could dream, Big Boy would be ringing her bell and sounding her whistle.

DONG-DONG-DONG-DONG-DONG-DONG

WHOOOOOO-WHOO-WHOOOOOO

If steam locomotives could dream, Big Boy would be chugging up the Wasatch Mountains at top speed, feeling the warmth of the coal in her firebox, as powerful as 7,000 horses.

But Big Boy 4014, the largest steam locomotive in the world, sat stranded. She sat almost a mile from the nearest train track, at an outdoor museum in Pomona, California.

She had been there over half a century.

Cold ashes lay in her firebox.

Cobwebs wove through her wheels.

Rust crept into her cab.

People came from around the world to visit and to marvel.

The Big Boys were part of history. In the beginning, there were 25 of them.

The Union Pacific Railroad had them built to carry heavy freight across the Wasatch Mountains. During World War II, they carried American soldiers and military equipment across the western prairies. Big Boys helped win the war.

That was a long time ago. Only eight were saved from the scrap heap.

One day, in the summer of 2013, visitors came whose conversations were different.

Impossible!

She's a giant, for sure.

It will cost a fortune to rebuild her.

What a crazy idea.

Even if it can be done, where would she run?

*She'll **never** run again.*

If steam locomotives could hope, Big Boy would hope for a great Steam Team.

If steam locomotives could hope, Big Boy would hope to be on the tracks again, rolling past grasslands and sagebrush, her whistle echoing through the mountains.

ChugaChuga . . . ChugaChuga . . . ChugaChuga . . . ChugaChug
DONG-DONG-DONG-DONG-DONG-DONG
WHOOOOOO-WHOO-WHOOOOOO

Nine men made up the Steam Team.

They aimed to restore Big Boy for the Golden Spike Celebration, the 150th anniversary of the completion of the transcontinental railroad. That was the first railroad to stretch across the North American continent.

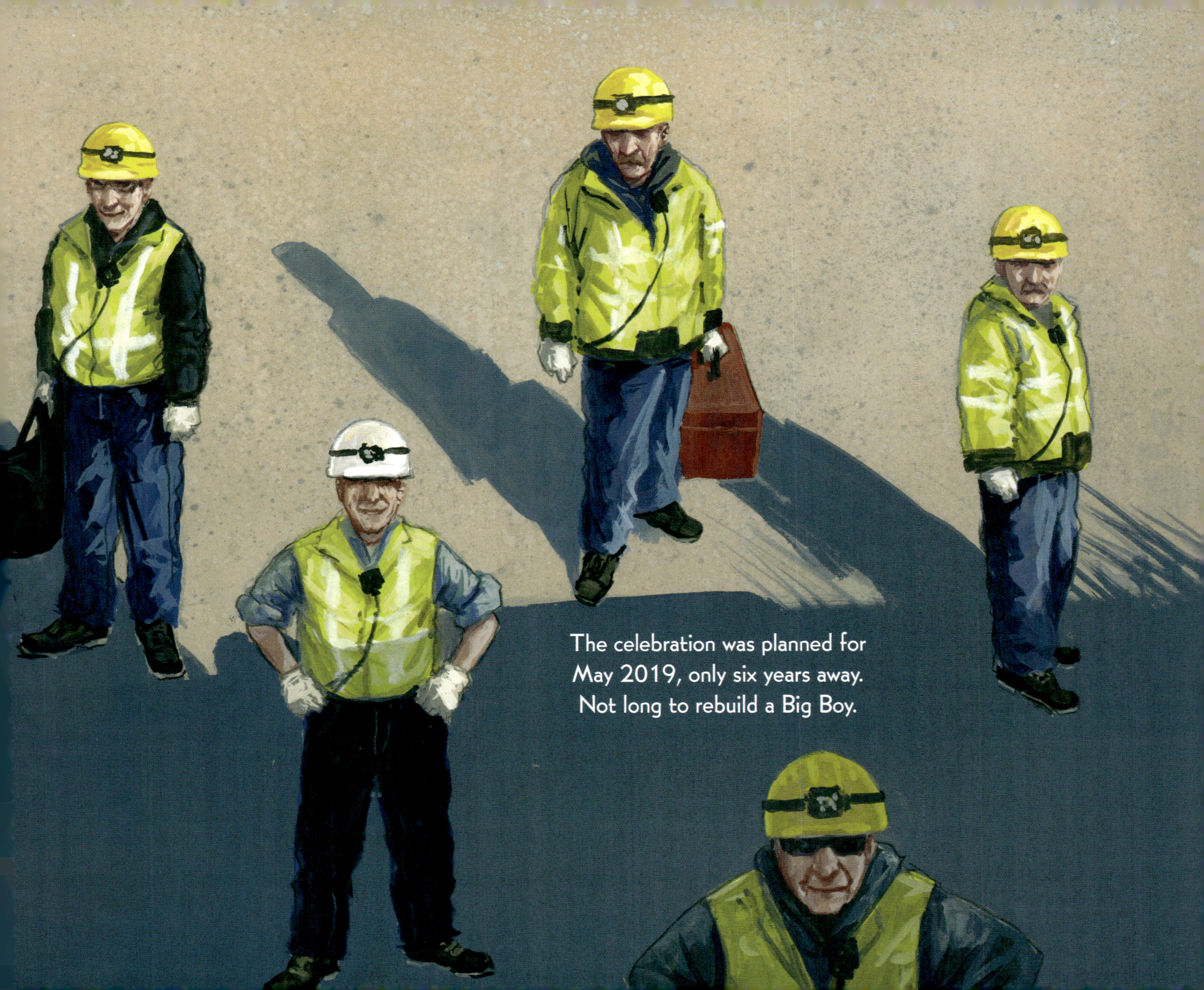

The celebration was planned for May 2019, only six years away. Not long to rebuild a Big Boy.

The train track was almost a mile from where Big Boy sat at the Los Angeles County fairgrounds. How could they move Big Boy without any track?

They would build it!

After temporary tracks were laid, a giant earthmover dragged Big Boy backward, inch by inch, across the fairground parking lot.

Inch by inch . . .

inch by inch . . .

until Big Boy reached the main rail line.

Two modern diesel locomotives moved Big Boy nearly 1,300 miles, from Los Angeles to Cheyenne, Wyoming, where she would be restored. One hauled. One pushed.

Hauled and pushed.

Hauled and pushed.

They hauled and pushed all the way to Cheyenne,
where Big Boy was tucked into the Union Pacific Steam Shop.

When the Steam Team was ready to disassemble and rebuild her,
they put Big Boy on a turntable and gave her a spin to take a look.
Then they moved her back into the Steam Shop and got to work.

First preparation. Then restoration.

Take the mighty Big Boy apart.
If a piece was worn-out,
the Steam Team made it brand-new.

Test those bolts. Check those rivets.

Grab the torches. Grab the welders.

All new valves. All new pistons.

Take out the ashpan and coal-burning grates.

Put in a fire pan and new oil burner.

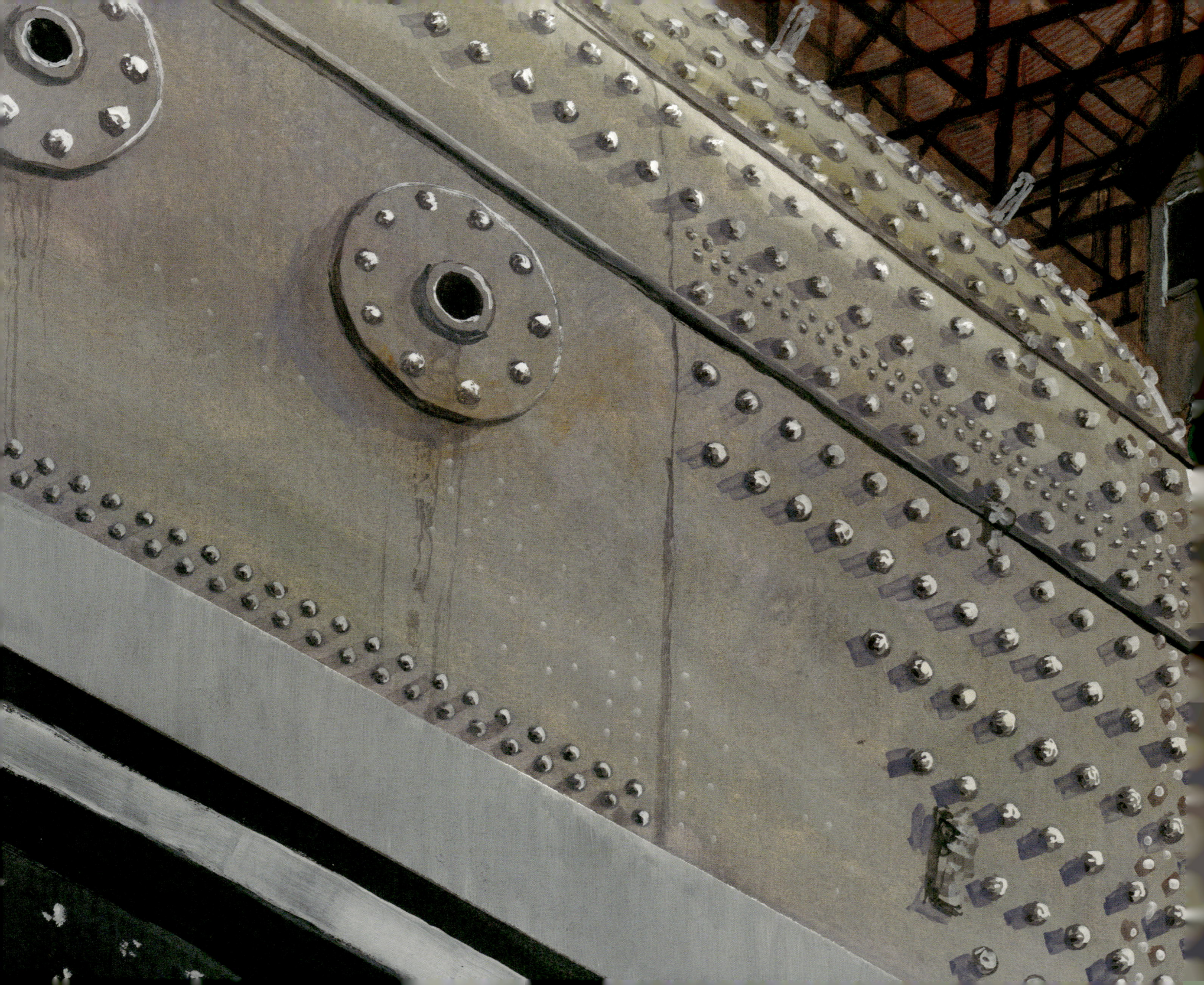

Time to put her back together again.

Paint that old cab green.

Make her look like new.

Two *months* to the Golden Spike Celebration.

Two *days* to the Golden Spike Celebration!

After years of planning, preparing, and restoration, the impossible was DONE.

If steam locomotives could feel, Big Boy 4014 would be thankful for her Steam Team.

Fire her up.

Test her out.

On May 1, 2019, Big Boy moved under her own power for the first time in nearly 60 years. The next day was her official test run, into Colorado and back.

She was ready!

Big Boy double-headed with the "Living Legend," locomotive 844, to Ogden, Utah, for the celebration. Two engines for a double dose of power.

People lined the tracks to feel the rumble under their feet as Big Boy passed, to see the steam cloud billowing above her, to hear her whistle, loud and clear.

On May 9, Big Boy 4014 arrived at the Golden Spike ceremony. Big Boy 4014 and locomotive 844 faced nose to nose, replicating two locomotives that had faced each other 150 years before. That was when a golden spike had united two railroads, making them one.

People came from around the world. Cameras clicked. Children cheered. Dignitaries made speeches.

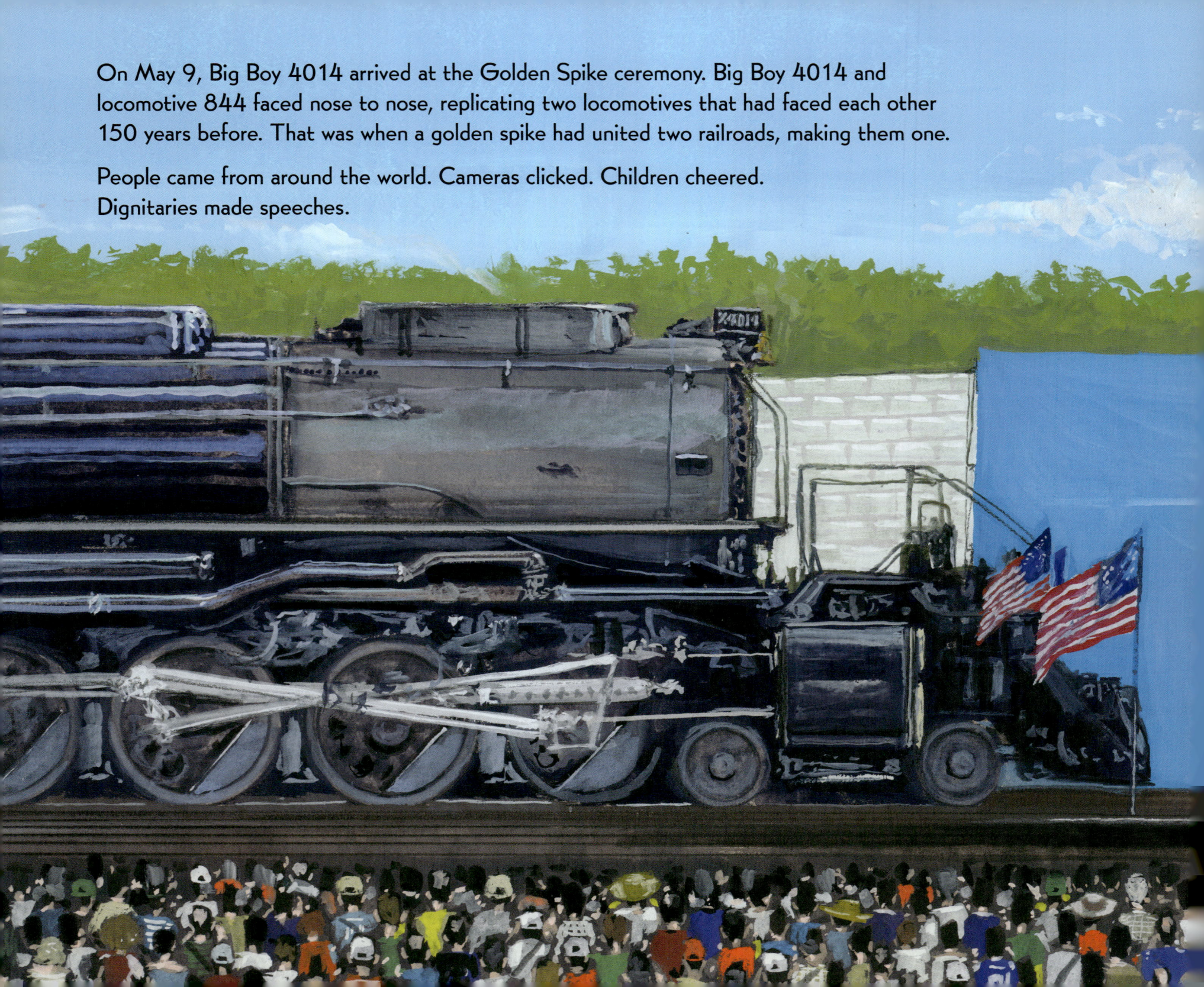

Still, the best was yet to come.

Now that the Steam Team knew Big Boy could travel the rails, they planned more tours so more people could see her.

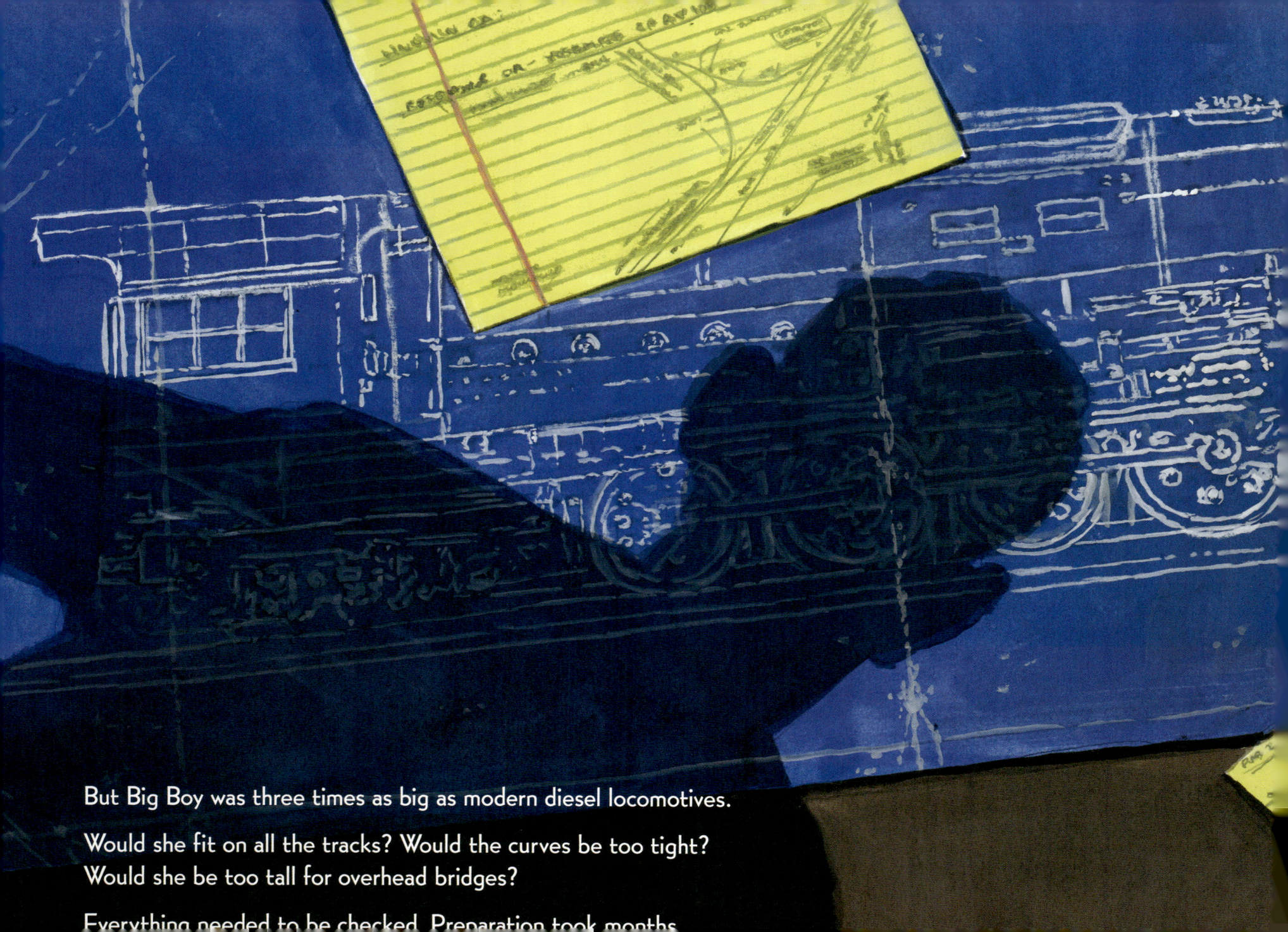

But Big Boy was three times as big as modern diesel locomotives.

Would she fit on all the tracks? Would the curves be too tight?
Would she be too tall for overhead bridges?

Everything needed to be checked. Preparation took months.

The first tour, in July and August of 2019,
took Big Boy over 8,000 miles.

Past grasslands and sagebrush.

Past farmlands and rivers.

Past fields and cities and towns.

On rainy days, people came to see her.

On sweltering hot days, people came to see her.

No matter the weather, they came to watch as Big Boy steamed by. Some smiled. Some cheered. Some wept, having thought they'd never see a Big Boy on the rails again, never feel the earth shiver as she passed by.

If steam locomotives could talk, Big Boy would say, "Thank you for coming. Stand 25 feet back! My steam is hot."

"I'm pulling out of the station now."

ChugaChuga . . . ChugaChuga . . . ChugaChuga . . . ChugaChug

"I'm ringing my bell and sounding my whistle."

DONG-DONG-DONG-DONG-DONG-DONG

WHOOOOOO-WHOO-WHOOOOOO

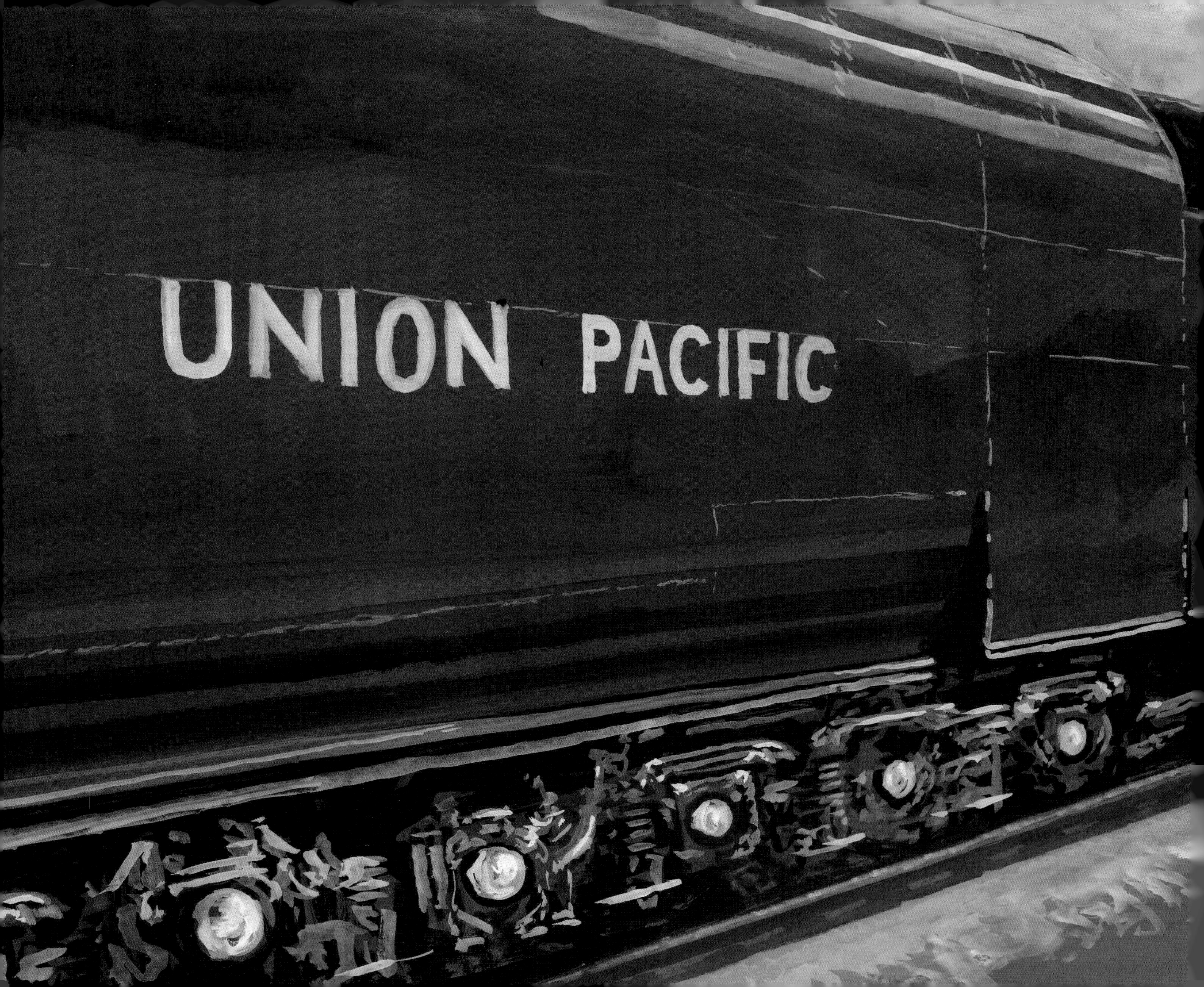
UNION PACIFIC

"I'm chugging up the Wasatch Mountains at top speed, feeling the warmth of the oil in my firebox, as powerful as 7,000 horses."

AUTHOR'S NOTE

Before the Big Boys, trains had to climb steep uphill slopes when traveling over the Wasatch Mountains in Utah. This often required double-heading, two locomotives pulling together, one behind the other. Double-heading provided more power but slowed service. The president of the Union Pacific Railroad, William Jeffers, wanted a locomotive that could haul 3,600 tons all by itself. In 1940, he asked Union Pacific's Vice President, Otto Jabelmann, to develop such a locomotive. That's when the Big Boys were built.

Union Pacific is a railroad company that was established in 1862 under President Abraham Lincoln. It carries freight across 23 states in the Western and Midwestern United States. It has supported Americans during war and hardship. More than any other railroad, Union Pacific has honored its past in ways like maintaining its Heritage Fleet, their collection of historic locomotives, one of which is Big Boy No. 4014.

Between 1941 and 1944, 25 Big Boys were built for Union Pacific at the American Locomotive Company in New York. That's where they got their name. A worker wrote *Big Boy* in chalk on the first Big Boy 4000's smokebox. The name stuck.

Because they were so long and big, the Big Boys' frames were articulated. They were like two engine units moving independently. The front engine was connected by a large special connection that allowed the Big Boys to travel around curves more easily. The Big Boys also had a unique wheel arrangement (4-8-8-4): four wheels that guided the engine; eight driving wheels; eight *more* driving wheels; then four wheels to support the rear of the locomotive.

A tender car rides behind Big Boy 4014 with a fuel supply and a big water tank. Big Boy 4014's original fuel was coal, but it's oil now. The oil flows by gravity from the tender into the firebox. The water tank supplies water to Big Boy's boiler. The fire in the firebox heats the water in the boiler, which turns into steam. That steam pushes pistons back and forth, making the *chug-chug* sound. Those pistons move the wheels. You can see the steam coming out of the double smokestacks in big white puffs.

After traveling more than one million miles over 18 years of service, Big Boy 4014 pulled her last train in 1959. Less expensive diesel-electric power had become popular. Of the 25 Big Boys built, 17 were scrapped, leaving 8 to go to museums and other venues in the United States where people could come to see them.

For most of its retirement, Big Boy 4014 was at the RailGiants Train Museum in Pomona, California. In 1961, it was gifted by the Union Pacific Railroad to the Southern California chapter of the Railway & Locomotive Historical Society. It was on display at the Los Angeles County fairgrounds from 1962 to 2013.

Steam locomotive fans from around the world thought a Big Boy would never roll on the rails again. But in 2013, Union Pacific made plans to return Big Boy 4014 to its Steam Shop in Cheyenne, Wyoming, and restore her. It was chosen over the other seven remaining locomotives

Big Boy 4014

PHOTO © UNION PACIFIC RAILROAD

for a few reasons. Southern California was a good place to keep a locomotive. The dry desert climate helped reduce rust. Also, the RailGiants Train Museum, along with two volunteers, Paul Guercio and Rick Brown, had kept Big Boy 4014 lubricated and cleaned over the years. Over a two-week period in April and May 2014, two modern freight diesels towed Big Boy 4014 back to Cheyenne, Wyoming, where she was restored and converted from burning coal to burning oil.

It was Ed Dickens who selected Big Boy 4014 to be restored. Mr. Dickens is Manager of Union Pacific's Heritage Operations, responsible for restoring and operating the steam locomotives in Union Pacific's Heritage Fleet, including Big Boy 4014. He is the engineer who has operated Big Boy 4014 on all her modern excursions. He and the Big Boy Steam Team are rock stars to railfans around the world. They all grew up loving trains and are experts in maintaining and operating steam locomotives.

During the restoration, Union Pacific decided to send Big Boy 4014 to the 2019 Golden Spike Celebration. The Golden Spike Celebration observed the 150th anniversary of the building of the transcontinental railroad, which had joined the Central Pacific Railroad to the Union Pacific Railroad. In 1863, the Central Pacific Railroad started laying track in California. In 1865, the Union Pacific Railroad started laying track in Nebraska. Railroad track was laid over 2,000 miles of rugged land. The railroad was built almost entirely by hand and took six years. Workers included many nationalities, ethnicities, and religions. The last track was laid in 1869 at Promontory Summit, Utah, where the golden spike was hammered into the final tie. The spike was real gold, 17.6 karat. After the ceremony, the spike was removed from the track and is now in Stanford University's Cantor Arts Center.

On May 4, 2019, Big Boy 4014 made her first run from Cheyenne, Wyoming, to Ogden, Utah, for the Golden Spike Celebration. She double-headed with "Living Legend" steam locomotive 844 on that "Great Race to Ogden."

Union Pacific Railroad has sponsored other tours to celebrate Big Boy 4014 and to honor the railroad's employees and the communities it serves. Because of Big Boy's size, months of planning are required to prepare for these tours. Ed Dickens is the one who checks every track Big Boy plans to travel. He looks at clearances and overhead bridges. He makes sure curves are not too tight. For "The Great Tour Across the Midwest," in 2019, he took an 11,000-mile planning trip before operating Big Boy on the tracks.

Millions of people have come to see Big Boy 4014 on the rails since she was restored. Thanks to Union Pacific Railroad's Robynn Tysver, I was invited to ride in Big Boy's cab with Ed Dickens. Thanks to my husband, Fred Arnold, I was there! He drove me from our home in Florida, to Omaha, Nebraska, for the "Home Run Express" tour. There I marveled at Big Boy 4014 and even gave her a hug.

More tours will be planned in the future. Many railfans look forward to seeing Big Boy 4014 rumble past, as powerful as 7,000 horses.

Marsha Diane Arnold and Big Boy 4014

Gratitude and thanks to the Steam Team

Ed Dickens, Manager of Union Pacific's Heritage Operations

Mr. Dickens is a steam locomotive engineer and mechanic

who helps maintain the Union Pacific Railroad's historic steam and diesel fleet, including

Big Boy 4014.

Jimmy Thompson, Kirt Clark, Garland Baker, Austin Barker,

Ted Schulte, Bruce Kirk, Troy Plagge, Don Crerar

Amazing Statistics about Big Boy No. 4014, the world's largest operating steam locomotive

Length—132 feet long with tender

Weight—1.2 million pounds (600 tons)

Height—16 feet, 2 inches

Width—11 feet

Cost of building—$265,000 in 1941. This would be about $5.5 million today.

SELECTED BIBLIOGRAPHY

BOOKS

Zimmermann, Karl. *Steam Locomotives: Whistling, Chugging, Smoking Iron Horses of the Past*. Honesdale, PA: Boyds Mills Press, 2004.
Wrinn, Jim, compiler. *Union Pacific's Big Boys: The Complete Story from History to Restoration*. Waukesha, WI: Kalmbach Media, 2020.

MAGAZINES

"How Union Pacific Did the Impossible! Big Boy Back in Steam." *Trains* magazine. Kalmbach Media, 2019.

DVDS

Trains–Big Boy Back in Steam: 4014's Triumphant Return. Kalmbach Media, 2019.
Trains–Big Boy on Tour 2019 Part II: 4014 in the Midwest, Southwest, South. Kalmbach Media, 2020.

I enjoyed many websites and YouTube videos while researching Big Boy's story.
Numerous videos of Big Boy 4014 traveling the rails and on tours can be found there.

INFORMATION CAN ALSO BE FOUND AT

Union Pacific Steam Program and RailGiants Train Museum